3
4.7

CANOES & KAYAKS

BOATS & SHIPS

Jason Cooper

The Rourke Corporation, Inc.
Vero Beach, Florida 32964

PHOTO CREDITS:
© Francis E. Caldwell/Affordable Photo Stock: page 12, page 18; © Jerry Hennen: title page, pages 7, 8, 10, 15; © Lynn M. Stone: pages 4, 13; courtesy Wenonah Canoe: pages 17, 21

CREATIVE SERVICES:
East Coast Studios, Merritt Island, Florida

EDITORIAL SERVICES:
Susan Albury

Library of Congress Cataloging-in-Publication Data

Cooper, Jason, 1942-
    Canoes and kayaks / by Jason Cooper.
        p. cm. — (Boats)
    Includes index.
    Summary: Describes the history, uses, and parts of canoes and kayaks and the paddling techniques of canoeing and kayaking.
        ISBN 0-86593-560-2
        1. Canoes and canoeing—Juvenile literature. 2. Kayaking—Juvenile literature. 3. Kayaks—Juvenile literature.
[1. Canoes and canoeing. 2. Kayaks and kayaking.]
I. Title II. Series: Cooper, Jason, 1942- Boats & ships
GV784.3.C66   1999
623.8'29—dc21   99–15110
                                                              CIP

Printed in the USA

TABLE OF CONTENTS

CANOES AND KAYAKS

Boats take people on adventures to places where they might not otherwise go. Kayaks (KIE aks) and canoes (kuh NOOZ) are especially good for adventure. They carry people on waterways that bigger, heavier boats can't. And they're light enough to be carried over land from one lake or stream to another.

With a kayak or canoe, a paddler not only sees the sights, he or she hears them. Canoes and kayaks rarely use an engine, so they are quiet. People in these boats enjoy the sounds of nature. Canoes and kayaks don't frighten wild animals as easily as motorboats do.

A kayak or canoe can take you on outdoor adventures in out-of-the-way places. This kayak can float in just inches of water.

Canoes and kayaks are long, narrow, lightweight boats. Some can be equipped with a small sail or engine. But canoes and kayaks are largely do-it-yourself boats. Either the paddlers or the water **current** (KUHR unt) makes the boat go.

Paddles are long handles with broad, flat ends, shaped roughly like a beaver tail. A canoe paddle has a blade on one end. A kayak paddle has a blade at each end.

Kayakers and canoeists can enjoy the sounds as well as the sights of nature from their quiet craft.

CANOES

The **hull** (HUHL) of any boat is its floating shell. A canoe is basically just that—a narrow, uncovered hull with a pointed front or bow (BOW) and usually a pointed back or stern (STURN).

The U-shaped hull is supported by U-shaped structures called **ribs** (RIBZ). The ribs follow the shape of the hull.

Thwarts (THWORTS) support the hull by stretching across the open top of the canoe.

Most canoes are 11 to 20 feet (3.4-6.1 meters) long and 35 to 40 inches (89-102 centimeters) wide. They are just 12 to 14 inches (30-36 centimeters) deep. A canoeist sits close to the water!

Canoeists quietly float past the cliffs of Labyrinth Canyon on the Green River.

CANOEING

A canoeist rides on a flat seat that reaches across the hull. Or the canoeist may kneel on the floor of the canoe.

Paddling a canoe requires strength and skill. The amount of each needed depends upon where the canoeist wishes to travel.

Some canoes are designed for one or two paddlers. Large freight canoes carry several people.

Canoes can be paddled and controlled on still water quite easily. Fast-moving or rough water requires much more skill. Canoes tip over without much help.

A canoeist should always wear a **life jacket** (LIFE JAK uht) and know the water and weather where he or she travels.

Canoeists paddle on a lazy river. They work together to keep the canoe on a straight course.

A kayak bobs in the white water of the Elwha River of Olympic National Park in Washington. Whitewater kayakers wear helmets as well as life jackets.

Kayakers watch the dorsal fin of a killer whale in British Columbia. The kayakers are safe. The whales are chasing salmon, not kayaks.

THE FIRST CANOES

The first canoes were not the smooth, sleek craft that come out of factories today. They were tree trunks that had their insides cut out to make them hollow.

A more modern canoe was crafted by Native Americans. They peeled sheets of bark from paper birch trees. By attaching bark to a wooden frame, they made canoes. Today's canoe design is similar, but the building materials have changed.

Modern canoes are made of fiberglass, plastic, canvas, **aluminum** (uh LOO muh num), or a material that can be air-filled. A few canoes are made of wood.

At Old Fort Williams in Ontario, canoes are made in the old-fashioned way— from birch bark.

KAYAKS

Since a canoe hull is usually open, a canoeist can sit in a normal sitting position, as if he or she were on a chair.

The kayak's hull is covered. The only uncovered space is an opening in the cover called the **cockpit** (KAHK pit).

This is where the kayaker sits, almost on the floor of the kayak. The kayaker's legs are outstretched on the kayak floor.

Some kayaks have two or more cockpits.

The bungee cords on the bow of this kayak can be used to tie down gear that won't fit in the cockpit.

A kayaker may wear a **spray skirt** (SPRAY skurt) to keep water out of the cockpit. The plastic spray skirt fits around the kayaker's waist and attaches to the sides of the cockpit.

Kayaks measure from 11 to 30 feet (3.4-9 meters). They weigh 25 to 75 pounds (11.3-34 kilograms) and are 20 to 35 inches (51-89 centimeters) across.

Kayaks can be made of fiberglass, plastic, or fabric. A few types made of fabric can be collapsed or filled with air.

Some kayaks are quite sturdy afloat, but others, like canoes, are tipsy.

A popular type of kayak is the lightweight inflatable. It can be filled with air. This kayak weighs just 13 pounds (6 kilograms).

KAYAKING

The open hulls of canoes are not suited for ocean paddling. But sea kayaks, with their covered hulls, are at home in salt water. At least two kayakers have crossed the Atlantic Ocean. Another kayaker, Ed Gilbert, paddled from California to Hawaii—by himself!

The kayak began as a seacraft. Its inventors were North American Inuit. They built kayaks of caribou and seal skins to hunt and fish in the Arctic seas.

A kayaker sits in the cockpit of his kayak at sea. A kayak moves forward when the kayaker dips and digs one blade into the water, then the other.

WHERE CANOES AND KAYAKS GO

Kayaks and canoes in skilled hands can explore wonderful out-of-the-way places.

The fast, rough stretches of tumbling river called **white water** (HWITE WAH tur) lure some kayakers and canoeists. Kayaks can handle rougher white water than open canoes.

Kayakers can be seen paddling among the coves and fingers of sea coasts. In British Columbia, kayakers quietly glide among pods of feeding killer whales (orcas).

Canoes are ideal for exploring wilderness lakes and lazy rivers.

GLOSSARY

aluminum (uh LOO muh num) — a strong, lightweight metal often used in airplane frames

cockpit (KAHK pit) — the opening in the deck where a kayaker sits

current (KUHR unt) — the natural movement or flow of water in a river or stream

hull (HUHL) — the floating shell of a boat or ship

life jacket (LIFE JAK uht) — a vest-like object that wraps around a person's chest and will keep the person afloat

rib (RIB) — one of many matching U-shaped structures built into a canoe hull for support

spray skirt (SPRAY skurt) — the plastic sheet that covers the opening between kayakers and the sides of their cockpit

thwart (THWORT) — the braces across the top of a canoe hull, including the seats

white water (HWITE WAH tur) — water that appears white as it rushes over or between rocks; stretches of river rapids

INDEX

FURTHER READING

Find out more about canoes and kayaks with these helpful books and information sources:

• American Canoe Association, 7432 Alban Station Boulevard, Suite B232, Springfield, VA 22150; on line at www.aca-paddler.org
• Armentrout, David. *Boating.* Rourke, 1998